THE TRUTH OF DEMOCRACY

To Patrick Lannan—

Thank you for all
you do for Santa Fe
and for égal liberté.

Sheridan Phillips

just ideas

transformative ideals of justice in ethical and political thought

series editors

Drucilla Cornell

Robert Berkowitz

Kenneth Panfilio

THE TRUTH OF DEMOCRACY

Jean-Luc Nancy

Translated by Pascale-Anne Brault and Michael Naas

FORDHAM UNIVERSITY PRESS

NEW YORK 2010

The Truth of Democracy was first published in French as *Vérité de la démocratie* by Jean-Luc Nancy © Editions Galilée, 2008.

Library of Congress Cataloging-in-Publication Data

Nancy, Jean-Luc.
    [Vérité de la démocratie. English]
    The truth of democracy / Jean-Luc Nancy ; translated by Pascale-Anne Brault and Michael Naas. — 1st ed.
        p.   cm. — (Just ideas)
    Includes bibliographical references.
    ISBN 978-0-8232-3244-4 (cloth : alk. paper) — ISBN 978-0-8232-3245-1 (pbk. : alk. paper) — ISBN 978-0-8232-3246-8 (ebook)
    1. Democracy.   2. Democracy—France.   3. Student movements—France—History—20th century.   4. Protest movements—France—History—20th century.   I. Title.
JC423.N32514   2010
321.8—dc22

                                                                    2010010931

Printed in the United States of America
12 11 10   5 4 3 2 1
First edition

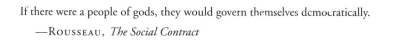

If there were a people of gods, they would govern themselves democratically.
—ROUSSEAU, *The Social Contract*

Contents

Translators' Note

Pascale-Anne Brault and Michael Naas

The Truth of Democracy comprises three texts written by Jean-Luc Nancy over a period of nine years on the questions of the meaning, truth, and future of democracy. The first and longest of the three, "The Truth of Democracy," was written early in 2008 (and published by Éditions Galilée later in the same year) to commemorate the fortieth anniversary of May 1968. In this text Nancy demonstrates how this extraordinary and still controversial time in French history radically transformed our thinking of politics and democracy. The second essay, "The Senses of Democracy," written in December 1999, takes a look back at various meanings or senses of democracy (from Rousseau to Tocqueville and Marx), before offering its own unique definition of democracy in relationship to these earlier ones. The final text, "Is Everything Political?" written in April 2000, takes up many of the same themes as the first two in order to focus on the question of whether politics in general or democratic politics in particular must always propose a totalizing vision for a people, a nation, or mankind as a whole, or whether it might entail precisely a detotalization that offers no such vision or ideal for either the state or for man but instead opens the space of the political and constitutes what Nancy calls man's "being in common."

Written in a direct and accessible, almost manifestolike style, this collection presents a forceful plea to rethink democracy not as one political regime or form among others but as that which opens and leaves open the very experience of being in common. With little direct citation or in-depth analysis of other thinkers on the topic, *The Truth of Democracy* creates its own context and can fruitfully be read on its own terms as a significant rethinking of the ideas and ideals commonly associated with democracy (freedom, equality, sovereignty, and so on). But this collection is perhaps even more intriguing and rewarding when read against the backdrop of Nancy's earlier works, from *The Inoperative Community* and the *Experience of Freedom* to *The Sense of the World*, to name just three. Those familiar with Nancy's work will thus recognize here many of Nancy's favorite themes and terms—community, communism, being in common, *partage* (as "sharing [out],)", singularity and the singular-plural, "sense" (as both meaning and direction), world, freedom, and, of course, democracy. Many of the thinkers whom Nancy has treated elsewhere are also evoked here (from Aristotle, Pascal, and Rousseau to Marx, Benjamin, and Derrida), but these proper names function more as signposts to punctuate the essay and point to other works in Nancy's corpus. By rearticulating the themes and terms he has developed elsewhere in relationship to an original analysis of what was and still is at stake in May 68, *The Truth of Democracy* is at once an eloquent summary of much of Nancy's work, indeed something of a primer for it, and a significant development of that work.

The initial provocation for the first of the three essays gathered here appears to be not only the fortieth anniversary of May 68 but some of the recent criticisms (some by French President Nicolas Sarkozy himself) leveled against the ideals and actors at the center of this important but still misunderstood moment in French history. Nancy here defends what he calls simply "68" without apology or equivocation, calling it an essential stage in the search for the "truth of democracy." Less a period within time (*chronos*) than a critical moment or interruption of time (*kairos*), 68 needs to be understood, Nancy argues, as an event or occurrence that provided a glimpse into the very "spirit of democracy," a spirit that is linked not to some common vision, idea, or desire (such as the Nation, the Republic, the People, or Humanity) but to an incommensurability (the infinity of man or man's exceeding of himself) at the origin of democracy.

Referring throughout to Pascal's notion that "man infinitely transcends man," Nancy argues that democracy must be founded upon a notion of freedom that is based not, as it traditionally is, upon the mastery and sovereignty of an autonomous subject but upon an exposure to this excess of man over himself. In the final analysis, democracy is nothing other than this opening of each to the other in an experience of inequality or incommensurability that subsequent political regimes and ideals (for example, liberal individualism) and economic systems (capitalism) have occluded by means of an equivalence between individuals and an absolute convertibility of values. Without a recognition of the infinite value of man (Marx) or the excess of man over himself (Pascal), democracy risks becoming conflated with or simply subsumed by these various modes of general equivalence and by governmental regimes that do little more than regulate competing interests and market forces. The "truth of democracy" thus lies not in a general equivalence between individuals but in what Nancy characterizes as a "communism" or a common being together in the world that exposes singularities to one another through art, love, friendship, thought, and so on—but not, importantly, through politics.

Democracy is thus not one political regime among others. Without any fundamental or essential form or figure, it must not subsume other authorities within it and cannot itself be subsumed by any other authority or institution, whether religious, scientific, aesthetic, or political. Democracy must therefore be thought as the incommensurable sharing of existence that makes the political possible but can in no way be reduced to the political. As such, it is first of all a metaphysics and only afterwards a politics. It was May 68, Nancy argues, that demonstrated all this in an exemplary way and so deserves to be not simply remembered and commemorated but rethought and renewed.

Though Nancy's work has been and will continue to be written off by some in France and elsewhere as nostalgic or indeed utopian "May 68 Thought"—and this collection, as an explicit defense of 68, will be an exemplary target for such criticism—Nancy makes a very strong case that what might be characterized as utopian is in fact the most concrete and pressing reality, while what might be called nostalgic is actually the demand for a future that can never simply arrive in time but nonetheless conditions everything that happens within time. It is as if, forty years after being first scrawled across university walls and storefronts in France, one of the most famous slogans of May 68 had received in *The Truth of Democracy* its most eloquent and poignant theoretical elaboration: "Be realistic, demand the impossible!"

• • •

The translators would like to thank the College of Liberal Arts and Sciences at DePaul University, and especially Dean Charles Suchar, for generous support of this project.

THE TRUTH OF DEMOCRACY

Following the timid and myopic denunciations of certain intellectuals, the authority who presides over the French state took it upon himself to characterize "May 68" as the origin of a general abdication and a moral relativism, an indifference and social cynicism whose victims were at once the virtue of politics and that of a capitalism supposedly full of scruples.[1] The accusation is so outrageous in its own cynicism and so disingenuous in its scarcely veiled cunning that it is hardly worth taking the time to answer it. It remains, nonetheless, at once worrisome and significant that such a crude accusation could even have been dreamed up. Worrisome because of the hardships for which we are being prepared, and significant because of the point of attack: to accuse 68 of immorality is to keep intact the virtue of a good politics and the integrity of a good capitalism, both in the service of thrifty citizen-workers. But it was politics itself and capitalism itself that were really being addressed by the 68 movement. It was against a kind of managerial democracy that its vehemence was directed, and, even more, it was a questioning of the very truth of democracy that was ventured there.

The aim of what follows is to clarify and help develop that first venture.

68–08

There is a very close and very deep connection between the commemoration of the fortieth anniversary of 68 and the current flurry of interest, as witnessed by so many publications, around the question of democracy. Though we were unable truly or fully to recognize it at the time, 68 initiated a calling into question of democracy's self-assurance, which might have seemed to be bolstered by the progress of decolonization, by the growing authority of the representations of the "state of law" and of "human rights," and by the ever clearer call for a form of social justice whose models would not be based upon the presuppositions implied by the term *communism* in the limited sense in which it had come to be understood.

It is for this reason that there is an anniversary of 68 only in the sense that we can indeed celebrate forty years—the time for a coming of age that can still be concerned and adventurous—of a process, mutation, or impetus that, in that year of the "March 22 Movement," threw out but the first anticipatory signs and that today is at best still in its early stages.[2]

There is thus no reason to speak of a "legacy" of 68, whether one declares oneself, in a rather ridiculous way, to be in favor of doing away with it or whether one wants to make it bloom again by claiming to renew its supposed spring. There is no legacy, there was no death. Its spirit has never stopped living.

Sixty-eight was neither a revolution nor a reform movement (even though a whole series of reforms ensued); it was neither a protest nor a rebellion, neither a revolt nor an insurrection, even though one can find in it certain elements of all these postures, postulations, aspirations, and expectations. What constitutes the real singularity of 68 and has so naturally conferred upon it the right to wear its date as monogram and patronym—like, before it, 89, 48, or 17—can only be discerned by setting aside, at least partially or relatively, all these categories.[3]

What preceded 68 and gave it its fundamental condition of possibility—other conditions being provided by more limited circumstances, namely, a certain clinging to the past in France, inertia in Germany, the U. S. involvement in Vietnam—had been, to go right to the heart of the matter, a scarcely visible but insistent disappointment, the nagging sense that we had never recovered something whose triumphant return seemed to have been announced by the end of the Second World War, namely, democracy.

This amounts to saying that 68 was not only possible but necessary (to the extent, at least, that this concept can be invoked in history) for the following reason: while the Second World War had seemed to be but a regrettable interruption in the development of international law and in the burgeoning of a relative concord or concert, if not actually a consensus, in the world of democratic nations, all this was far from recovering its earlier rate of growth and far from reaffirming its convictions. On the contrary, uncertainty was silently undermining what at the same time was meant to be a great "reconstruction" effort, to use the term that served as the motto for the transformation of the CFDT[4]—emblematic of the democratic spirit of the time.

Inadequate Democracy

This age did not realize that it was slowly falling behind itself. Something within history was in the process of exceeding, overflowing, or diverting the principal flow of hopes and struggles that were the continuation of those of the previous two half centuries.

Europe could not see to what extent it was no longer what it had believed itself to be, or perhaps to what extent it could not become what it nonetheless endeavored to engender, that is, "Europe" as a spiritual entity and a geopolitical unity. At stake in the Cold War seemed to be a confrontation between different responses to the challenges posed by the history of the industrial and democratic world: one still conceived of the possibility of another subject in the course of events (in a progress that would be at once technological and social), a subject modeled on some other vision of man and his community, a vision for which there was no shortage of competing "third ways" or regulative ideas, at once postcolonial, postsoviet, and something more than "bourgeois" democracy. In different ways, the notions of the worker council or self-management, of direct democracy or permanent revolution, occupied a horizon whose possibilities remained linked to an organized if not organic action, to a planning process or prospective whose formal schema was even introduced into the conception of the state.

We didn't know that we were in the process of leaving "the age of world pictures" (to take up, quite deliberately, the title of a text in which Heidegger, in 1938, demonstrated quite clearly the closure of such an "age"), that is, the age of world conceptions, of fore-visions or fore-casts [*prévisions*] of a world transformed—reformed, renewed, indeed, recreated or refounded.[5]

So little did we know that we failed to recognize the importance of what had happened and was still happening in the name of what began to be called "totalitarianisms." For it is with this term, whose validity has often been discussed and whose generic character at least must remain subject to caution, that we became accustomed very early on—too early, too quickly, in fact, even before the invention of the word—to designate, on the one hand, an absolute political evil that is in opposition to democracy and, on the other, an evil that simply befell democracy, that came to it from out of nowhere, or from an outside already in itself bad (the perversity of some doctrine or else the madness of some individual). The thought that what had happened might be due to reasons and expectations arising out of democracies themselves, though not completely lacking at the time, was unable to lead to sufficient reflection upon what had made democracy inadequate to itself, be it the loss of a form once attained (as the proponents of republicanism claim) or else a constitutive lack in a democracy that did not know how to bring to light, that could not or did not want to bring to light, in truth, the *demos* that was supposed to be its principle.

A similar thought of the inadequacy of democracy (representative, formal, bourgeois) to its own Idea—and, as a result, at once to a truth of "the people" and to a truth of *kratein*, of power—had been present, and sometimes quite actively so, before the second and even the first "world" war. But this usually had the effect of actually feeding certain "totalitarian" movements or else, at the very least, of supporting a sort of fringe aura around some of them: it was impossible not to be either somewhat or completely "Marxist," even if in one of its sophisticated or aestheticized versions, or else it was necessary to be "revolutionary," even if in a "conservative" or "spiritual" way. In any case, thought turned away from democracy, able at the very most to consider it a lesser evil. But then democracy would inevitably bear within itself either the lie of exploitation or that of mediocrity, the two lies, moreover, being very easily combined. Democratic politics thus sank ineluctably into a double denial: of justice and of dignity.

Democracy Exposed

Democracy has thus been reevaluated since the Second World War less for itself than in opposition—and how vehement and justified this opposition was—to "totalitarianisms," the memory of which (with regard to fascisms) and the growing condemnation of which (with regard to Stalinisms) constantly invited us to turn our back on them. But this turning away did not lead to an awareness of the fact that the most significant political catastrophes of the middle of the century were not the result of the sudden emergence of inexplicable demons. The dominant explanatory schema remained barbarity, madness, betrayal, deviance, or malevolence; usually one ignored, less deliberately than somnambulistically, what could have been learned or inferred from the analyses of, say, Bataille or Benjamin, Arendt or . . . Tocqueville.

To put it in a very cursory way, we saw democracy being attacked, but we did not see that it had also exposed itself to attack and that it called out to be reinvented as much as defended such as it was. Sixty-eight was the first irruption of the demand for such a reinvention.

Before 68, the European left had been mobilized by the struggles for decolonization and by the search for a radical reform (of the extreme left or the social left) aimed at breaking with what was then called "real" communism, even though its reality was anything but communist. But these struggles for decolonization, just like these calls for a break, often masked through their very urgency and fervor that it was not enough to readjust a misguided or inadequate vision. They masked the fact that it would not be enough simply to rectify the image of the good subject of history.

During this same time, in fact, a profound mutation of thought was underway—thought understood here in its broadest and deepest sense, in its most active and operative sense as well: thought as a reflection on civilization, existence, and forms of evaluation. It was no doubt during this period that the Nietzschean call for a "transvaluation of all values" became truly effective, though not in the histrionic and sinister way it did under the Third Reich. And that is why, notwithstanding all the good and God-fearing souls, we were and we remain Nietzschean in this regard: that is, in a word, we are trying to clear a path for the way out of nihilism. We know that it is narrow and difficult, but it is open.

We embarked upon this way out of nihilism the moment we began to leave behind a confrontation between conceptions and evaluations that all secretly (and/or unbeknownst to themselves) shared a common reference, or the semblance of such a reference, simply to choices, to more or less subjective options, in a sort of general democratism of values. In truth, we were in the process of displacing the entire regime of thought that allowed for the confrontation of options. For we were exiting not only the time of "conceptions," "visions," or "images" of the world (*Weltbilder*) but the general regime in which a vision understood as a theoretical paradigm implied the sketching out of certain horizons, the determination of goals [*visées*] and an operative fore-sight [*pré-vision*]. In the midst of the profound upheavals caused by decolonization—accompanied, on the one hand, by the multiplication of socialist-revolutionary or socialist-republican models, and, on the other, by the tectonic mutations of thought and representations—we left the age of "History," as Levi-Strauss, Foucault, Deleuze, and Derrida all diagnosed very early on, while Sartre boldly attempted to formulate a new way of thinking the subject of social *praxis*.

Of the Subject of Democracy

It will thus not have been for nothing, this "68 thought," which some believed and some still believe they can simply write off with sarcasm. It was not just a game or the fantasy of a few "intellectuals" but a feeling, a disposition, indeed, a habitus or ethos that entered into public consciousness and ways of thinking. Combined with a lack of confidence in at least a certain representation of political parties and labor unions, this ethos tended to decouple political action from the commonly accepted framework for the exercising or the taking of power—be this through electoral means or insurrection—and from all reference to models or doctrines, or indeed to "ideologies," as one would soon be saying in a brand-new sense of the term, that is, as a way of designating a configuration of ideas, bodies of thought, and no longer the inverted reflection of the real.

In many ways—ways that were in fact very different, even opposed— one stripped bare the regime of the "conception" (the conception of the subject and the subject of conception, the mastery of action and the action of mastery, vision and prevision [*prévision*], the projection and production of men and their relationships) in order to open a new regime of thought: no longer the engendering of forms responsible for modeling some historical given that had itself been in some sense preformed—at the very least by the general notion of "progress" and the possibility of exercising some rational control over the course of events in the name of a certain reason—but the exposition of the objectives themselves ("man" or "humanism," "community" or "communism," "sense" or "realization") to a going beyond in principle: to that which no prediction or foresight [*prévision*] is able to exhaust insofar as it engages an infinity in actuality.[6]

There never was, in what was most living and most serious in this time of thought, any putting into crisis or destabilization of the subject to the advantage of some sort of machination of forces and objects, as some have taken to repeating. There was an opening of the "subject" to what Pascal already knew quite explicitly, Pascal who inaugurated this "modern" time—or however you want to call it—by striking or imprinting it with this formula, which is at once absolute injunction, promise, and risk: "Man infinitely transcends man."[7] The "subject," in this respect, the "subject" presumed to be a self-producing, self forming, autotelic being in itself, the subject of its own presupposition and its own foresight—this subject, whether individual or collective, found itself to be already surpassed by events.

It was this subject that was at the heart of democracy. Whether representative or direct, democracy has not yet clearly distinguished its "conceptions" from the presupposition of a subject that is master of its representations, volitions, and decisions. That is why it is legitimate to question the underlying reality of the electoral process as well as the "democracy of opinion polls." This does not mean that we must without any further consideration replace political representation with the presentation—that is, with the imposition—of the good or the destiny of a people or peoples.

Many ambiguities can arise today regarding the real or supposed self-critique of democracy. One can, indeed, turn democratic principles against themselves and take advantage of an obvious weakness in order to pervert "human rights." This can be seen, for example, when one characterizes as "racist" certain critiques aimed at particular religious beliefs or when, in the name of a "politically correct" "multiculturalism," one finds a way to justify the subordination of women. More insidiously still, one can distort free expression at its root by supporting forms of education and cultural life that are under the spell of superstitions. But these very real threats must not encourage democracies to forsake their own lucidity—quite the contrary.

The Potential of Being

Sixty-eight had precisely the merit of resisting the will to present and dictate a vision, one with a direction and objectives. (It had, in essence, this merit there where it was most properly "68," something that is bound to escape the notice of every simply sociohistorical or, worse, psychosociological gaze.)

One way of getting out of History had been—and this was the case even before the war—recourse to a thinking of "messianism" understood less as the advent or coming of a Savior or Supreme Judge than as the event of a rupture of and in History. A thinking of time itself as disjunction rather than continuity, as secession rather than succession. This recourse to messianic thought has been taken up again in recent years, in particular following certain propositions of Derrida. We will not reopen here the debate over what does or does not justify the use of this messianic vocabulary: it is enough to mark the general sense of what will have in any case functioned, in relationship to History and since the 1920s, as the reoccurring symptom of a demand, always felt anew, to substitute the event for any kind of advent. Sixty-eight did not at all resort to this "messianic" theme—not even duly qualified as "without messianism" or "without Messiah." But it is not illegitimate to try for a moment to see a "messianic inspiration" in 68, in the sense that, instead of developing and advancing visions and previsions, predictions and forecasts, models and forms, preference was given to greeting the present of an irruption or disruption that introduced no new figure, agency, or authority.

What is important, in this regard, is not the "antiauthoritarianism" and the liberating or libertine sense one associates with 68—and not without reason—for better or for worse; what is important is one sense of this truth, namely, that "authority" cannot be defined by any preexisting authorization (whether institutional, canonical, or based on some norm) but can only proceed from a desire that expresses itself or recognizes itself in it. There is no subjectivism, certainly no psychologism, in this desire, only the expression of a true possibility and thus of a true potential of being.

If democracy has a sense, it would be that of having available to it no identifiable authority proceeding from a place or impetus other than those of a desire—of a will, an awaiting, a thought—where what is expressed and recognized is a true possibility of being *all together, all and each one among all.* It has to be repeated yet again: it is not by chance that the words *communism* and *socialism* came to bear, after undergoing all kinds of distortions, the exigency and fervor that the word *democracy* itself was unable or was no longer able to nourish. Sixty-eight recalls this all at once, in the present of an affirmation that first of all wants to be freed from every identification.

The Infinite and the Common

Democracy has not sufficiently acknowledged that it must *also*, in some way, be "communist," for otherwise it would be but the management of necessities and expediencies, lacking in desire, that is, in spirit, in breath, in sense. It is thus not only a matter of catching hold of a "spirit of democracy" but first of all of thinking that "democracy" *is spirit* before being a political and social form, institution, or regime. What might appear inconsistent, indeed "spiritualist" and "idealist," in this proposition in fact contains, on the contrary, the most real, concrete, and pressing necessity.

If Rousseau's *contract* has a sense beyond the juridical and protective limits to which its now dated concept confines it, it is because it does not produce the principles of a common body that governs itself without also producing, first of all and more essentially, *an intelligent being and a man*, as his text literally puts it.

The spirit of democracy is nothing less than this: the breath of man, not the man of a humanism measured against the height of man as he is given—for where would one find this given? under what conditions? what status would it have?—but man who infinitely transcends man. What we have been lacking up until now is Pascal with Rousseau. Marx was close to bringing them together, for he knew that man produces himself and that this production is worth infinitely more than any measurable evaluation. And it is Marx who lent, without any hope of return, his name—his proper name, not the label "Marxism"—to the communist exigency, which, when thought in this way, helps us to understand how it could have resisted and obligated to the point of being confused with certain traps or false paths.

This exigency, this exigency of man, of the infinite, and of the common—the same one just declined, modulated, modalized—cannot be, by essence, determined or defined. There is here a share of the incalculable that is, no doubt, the share most resistant to appropriation by a culture of general calculation—the one named "capital." This share requires that one break with all predictive calculations, with all expectations of return. It is not that this rupture must annul all anticipation, preparation, and taking account of the most just measures (in both senses of this term). But what is infinite in the exigency must also find its place—as well as its time, its moment. For a time—brief, as it had to be—the time of 68 was less *chronos* than *kairos*: less duration and succession than opportunity and encounter, an advening without advent, without consecration, the coming *and* going of an apprehending of the present as the presence and co-presence of possibles. These possibles were themselves defined less as rights than as potentials, potentialities that were appreciated less for their "feasibility" than for the opening or the expansion of being that they offered as potentialities, without having to be subjected to an unconditional realization, to say nothing of a reification. On the contrary, the unconditional must *also*, in its "unrealizable" absoluteness, continue to play a part in the work that is carried out.

The Sharing (Out) of the Incalculable

Put in other terms, a more than the work, an unworking or an inoperativity, is central to the work of existence: what this work puts in common is not only of the order of exchangeable goods but of the order of the unexchangeable, of what is without value because it is outside all measurable value.

The share of what is without value—the share of the sharing (out) of the incalculable, which is thus, strictly speaking, unshareable—exceeds politics. While politics must make possible the existence of this share, while its task is to maintain an opening for it, to assure the conditions of access to it, it does not take responsibility for its content. The element in which the incalculable can be shared (out) goes by the names of art or love, friendship or thought, knowledge or emotion, but not politics—in any case, not democratic politics. For democratic politics refrains from laying claim to this sharing (out), even though it guarantees its exercise.

It is precisely the expectation of a political sharing (out) of the incalculable that leads to disappointment with democracy. We have remained prisoners of a vision of politics as the putting to work and activation of an absolute sharing (out): the destiny of a nation or a republic, the destiny of humanity, the truth of relation, the identity of the common.

In short, everything that might have seemed to be subsumed by the glories of monarchy and that various "totalitarianisms" wanted to replace with a literally demo-cratic glory: the absolute power of a people identified in its essence and in its living body, an indigenous people or a people of workers, the self-production and autochthony of a principle substituted for the princes of yesteryear.

We thus tend to forget that monarchies were of divine right only by allowing to subsist within them—but as if on the side, as if in the margins—at least one other principle of sharing (out) or subsumption: that of a divine authority or destination that was never simply conflated with political authority and its destination. In Islam, too, there was this distinction between the properly theological order and the properly political one. In truth, it was already a characteristic of the Greek origins of politics to separate two orders, and the civic religions of antiquity did not simply merge into or become confused with the initiations, ecstasies, or revelations for which they nevertheless sometimes made room.[8]

Politics is born in the separation between itself and another order, one that today's public spirit or mindset no longer considers divine, sacred, or inspired but which maintains its separation no less (through, as we said, art, love, thought, and so on)—a separation that might be said to be that of truth or of sense, of this sense of the world that is outside of the world, as Wittgenstein said: sense as an outside that is open right in the middle of the world, right in the middle of us and between us as our common sharing (out). This sense is not the conclusion of our existences; it does not subsume them under a signification but simply opens them to themselves, which is also to say, to one another.

Sixty-eight recovered—or experienced anew, in an unprecedented way—the sense of this sense: right next to politics, right up against it, but also against it, or through it.

The Infinite in the Finite

The birth of democracy came to be saddled with the forgetting we have just recalled. By imagining that monarchy assumed the entirety of the destiny—of the existence or the essence—of peoples, nations, or communities, the first thinking of democracy was bound to be disappointed with itself: if Rousseau resigns himself to thinking that democracy properly speaking (direct, immediate, spontaneous) would be good only for a people of gods, it is because of his invincible conviction that the people should be divine, that man should be divine, in other words, that the infinite should be given.

But an infinite that is given is not the infinite of Pascal's transcendence or going beyond. The infinite going beyond goes infinitely beyond itself. It is neither given nor to be given. It is not to be presented in a signification or under any identity. Which, nevertheless, does not prevent it from being infinite in actuality, an actual and not potential infinite: not the indefinite pursuit of an end that is perpetually receding, but actual, effective, and perduring presence. This does not mean that it is of the order of the measurable or even of the determinable in general. It is the presence of the infinite in the finite, the infinite open within the finite (which Derrida formulated in these terms: "Infinite différance is finite"—"différ*a*nce" being for him not "deferral" but, on the contrary, the absolute presence of the incommensurable).

The infinite should not be given, and man should not be (a) god. This lesson—so radical, in truth, insofar as it takes man at the root, as Marx wanted, a root that is in infinite excess over man—is the correlative lesson of the invention of democracy. And Marx, in the end, was not unaware that man infinitely exceeds man. He did not think it or formulate it in these terms, but what his thinking inevitably leads to is the notion that the (social) production of man by man is an infinite process—and as a result, more than a "process" or a progress. Marx knew (though we will not try to show this here) that man as a "whole" is an infinite, that "value" in the absolute sense (neither use value nor exchange value) is an infinite, and that the "way out of alienation" is an infinite. What we thus need is Pascal and Rousseau with Marx.

Not to forget that man is not god, that his assumption under an absolute does not present itself but takes place *hic et nunc*, in a presence that the "dignity of the person" and "human rights" can never themselves assure, even if one must never dissociate them from it; not to forget, therefore, that the "common," the *demos*, can be sovereign only under a condition that distinguishes it from the sovereign assumption of the state and from any political configuration whatsoever—*that* is the condition of democracy. And that is what we have been called to understand since 68.

Distinguished Politics

This does not define a politics. It does not even determine in a sufficient manner what the properly political field is to be. But it does at least keep at bay the slogan "everything is political," which will no doubt have been, contrary to all appearances, a perfectly neotheological slogan. Neither everything nor, of course, nothing, politics must be understood through a distinction from—and a relation with—that which cannot and must not be assumed by it, not, to be sure, because this should be assumed by some other activity (art or religion, love, subjectivity, thought . . .), but because this must be taken charge of by all and by each in ways that must remain diverse, indeed divergent, multiple, even heterogeneous.

While the democratico-socialist dream has been that politics disappear as a separate agency and return as the bearer of all spheres of existence (the young Marx expressed himself more or less in these terms), politics cannot but be separated. Not separated by a suspicion that keeps all "politicians" at arm's length, but separated in accordance with the essence of being in common, which has to do with not letting itself be hypostasized in any figure or signification.

It is by beginning with this consideration, which at first seems quite removed from political concerns, that one can sketch out the democratic contours of the latter. This implies that politics must be *distinguished* in both senses of the term—keeping it distinct and granting it the distinctions it is due: in particular, by ceasing to dilute the exercise of power and the symbols of power through a democratism of indistinction where everything and everyone would be on the same footing and at the same level. One of the most glaring signs of the democratic malaise is our inability to think power as anything other than an adversarial or malevolent agency, as the enemy of the people, or else as the indefinitely multiplied and dispersed reality of all possible relations of force. In the name of taking these "micropowers" into account, one forgets the specificity of (political) power *itself*, along with its proper and distinct destination.

But, in a general way, the democratic exigency confronts us with the task of distinction. And this task of distinction is nothing other than that which might clear a path for the way out of nihilism. For nihilism is nothing other than the nullification of distinctions, that is, the nullification of senses or values. Sense or value comes about only through difference: one sense is distinguished from the other like right from left, or sight from hearing, and one value is essentially nonequivalent to any other. What gave rise to the Nietzschean critique of "values" and the notorious weakness of "value philosophies" was the thought of values as given markers—ideal or normative—against the backdrop of an equivalence between the evaluative gestures themselves. But value is to be found first of all in the distinction of the gesture that evaluates it, that distinguishes and creates it. What we need is this apparent oxymoron: a Nietzschean democracy.

Nonequivalence

The democratic world developed in the context—to which it is linked from the origin—of general equivalence. This expression—again from Marx—designates not only the general leveling of all distinctions and the reduction of all forms of excellence through mediocratization—a theme that, as we know, runs throughout the Heideggerian analysis of the "they" (where one can locate one of the symptomatic impasses of philosophy confronted with democracy—and this without prejudicing in the least the rigorous analysis that is called for). It designates first of all money and commodification, that is, the very heart of capitalism. A very simple lesson must be drawn from this: capitalism, the capitalism in which or with which, or perhaps even *as* which, democracy was born, is before all else, in its very principle, the choice of a mode of evaluation, namely, equivalence. Capitalism is the result of a decision on the part of civilization: value *is* in equivalence. The technology that was also deployed in and as an effect of this decision—although the technological relation to the world is properly and originally that of man—is a technology subject to equivalence: the equivalence between all its possible ends, and even, in a way that is just as extreme as that brought about through money, that between ends and means.

Democracy can thus become, by extension, the name of an equivalence even more general than the one Marx spoke of: ends, means, values, senses, actions, works, persons . . . all of them exchangeable because none of them is related to anything that might distinguish it, because all of them are related to an exchange that, far from being a "sharing (out)" in accordance with the proper richness of this term, is but a substitution of roles or a permutation of places.

The destiny of democracy is linked to the possibility of a mutation in the paradigm of equivalence. The challenge is thus to introduce a new nonequivalence that would have nothing to do, of course, with the non-equivalence of economic domination (the basis of which remains equiv-alence) or with the nonequivalence of feudalisms or aristocracies, or of regimes of divine election or salvation, or of spiritualities, heroisms, or aestheticisms. It would not simply be a matter of introducing another system of differential values; it would be a matter of finding, of achieving, a sense of evaluation, of evaluative affirmation, that gives to each evalu-ating gesture—a decision of existence, of work, of bearing—the possi-bility of not being measured in advance by a given system but of being, on the contrary, each time the affirmation of a unique, incomparable, unsubstitutable "value" or "sense." Only this can displace what is called economic domination, which is but the effect of the fundamental deci-sion for equivalence.

Contrary to what is shown by liberal individualism, which produces nothing other than an equivalence between individuals—even when they are designated "human persons"—it is the affirmation of each that the common must make possible: but an affirmation that "holds" or has "value," precisely, only among everyone and in some way by everyone, that refers to everyone as the possibility and opening of the singular sense of each and of each relation. Only this provides the way out of ni-hilism: not the reactivation of values but the manifestation of all against a background where the "nothing" signifies that all have value incom-mensurably, absolutely, and infinitely.

The affirmation of incommensurable value can seem piously idealistic. It must be heard, however, as a reality principle: it does not lend itself to reverie and it does not propose a utopia, and not even a regulative idea;

it announces that it is from this absolute valuing that one must begin. Never from an "it's all the same," "it all has the same value [*tout se vaut*]"—men, cultures, words, beliefs—but always from a "nothing's the same," "nothing is equivalent to anything else [*rien ne s'équivaut*]" (except what is open to negotiation, and that can ultimately include everything). Each one—each singular "one" of one, of two, of many, of a people—is unique by virtue of a unicity or singularity that *obligates* infinitely and *obligates itself* or *owes it to itself* to be put into actuality, into work, or into labor. But, at the same time, strict equality is the regime where these incommensurables are shared (out).

A Space Formed for the Infinite

The condition of nonequivalent affirmation is political inasmuch as politics must prepare the space for it. But the affirmation itself is not political. It can be almost anything you like—existential, artistic, literary, dreamy, amorous, scientific, thoughtful, leisurely, playful, friendly, gastronomic, urban, and so on: politics subsumes none of these registers; it only gives them their space and possibility.

Politics sketches out nothing more than the contour, or the many contours, of an indetermination whose opening might allow these affirmations to take place. Politics does not affirm; it accedes to the claim of affirmation. It itself does not bear "sense" or "value"; instead it makes it possible for these to find a place and for that place not to be one where a signification is achieved, realized, and reified, a signification that might lay claim to being an accomplished figure of the political.

Democratic politics renounces giving itself a figure; it allows for a proliferation of figures—figures affirmed, invented, created, imagined, and so on. That is why the renunciation of Identification is not a pure asceticism and why it has nothing to do with courage or virtuous abstinence, both of which would continue to be thought on the basis of resignation or loss. Democratic politics opens the space for multiple identities and for their sharing (out), but it is not up to it to give itself a figure. That is what political courage today must learn to acknowledge.

The renunciation of every principal form of identification—whether it be borne by the image of a King, a Father, a God, a Nation, a Republic, a People, a Man, or a Humanity, or even a Democracy—does not contradict, indeed quite the contrary, the exigency of identification in the sense of the possibility for each and every one to identify him or herself (or as people like to say today "to take up a subject position") as having a place, a role, and a value—an inestimable value—in being together. What makes politics, what makes the *"good life"* by which Aristotle defines politics, is a "good" that is precisely not determined in any way, by any figure or under any concept.[9] Not even, as a result, by the figure or the concept of the polis. For the polis is only the place from where (rather than "where"), the place from which—though without leaving it, without leaving the world that conjoins cities, nations, peoples, and states—it is possible to sketch out, to paint, to dream, to sing, to think, to feel a "good life" that measures up incommensurably to the infinite that every "good" envelops.

Democracy is not figurable. Better, it is not by essence figural. That is perhaps the only sense, in the end, that can be given to it: it overthrows the assumption of the figuration of a destiny, of a truth of the common. But it imposes the configuration of common space in a way that opens up the greatest possible proliferation of forms that the infinite can take, figures of our affirmations and declarations of our desires.

What has been happening in art over the last fifty years demonstrates in a striking way just how real this exigency is. The more the democratic city renounces giving itself a figure, the more it abandons its symbols and its icons in a no doubt risky fashion, the more it witnesses the emergence of all possible aspirations toward new and unprecedented forms. Art turns every which way in an attempt to give birth to forms that it would wish to be in excess of all the forms of what is called "art," and in excess of the very form or idea of "art." Whether we are talking about rock or rap, electronic music, videos, computer-generated images, tagging, art installations or performance art, or else new interpretations of older forms (such as drawing or epic poetry), everything bears witness to

a feverish anticipation, to a need to seize anew an existence in full transformation. If there is, as one says, a "crisis" of the novel, it is because we
still have to invent a new narrative for our history, henceforth deprived
of History. And if there is body art—to the point of blood, to the point
of suffering—it is because our bodies desire to understand themselves
differently. And the fact that this happens through every possible ec-
centricity or aberration is not a good enough explanation, for it also
happens through every possible exigency and appeal. One must learn
how to listen.

But all this poses anew the question of what the city as such must do
in this regard. It is not up to it either to take responsibility for the form
or the narrative or else to consider itself free of any obligation with
respect to it. It is a dilemma, to be sure, that is displayed in the most dis-
tressing way by the ambiguities of "cultural politics"—ambiguities on the
part of those who manage them and those who claim them. There is no
easy answer, perhaps no "answer" at all. But one must set to work, and
one must know that democracy is not an assumption of politics at work.

Praxis

Someone will say to me: So you are declaring openly that, for you, democracy is not political! And then you just leave us hanging, without any means of action, intervention, or struggle, as you gaze off dreamily toward your "infinite" . . .

But it's really quite the opposite. I in fact maintain that the political question can no longer seriously be asked except by considering what democracy engages as a sort of principial going beyond of the political order—but a going beyond that takes place only by starting from the polis, from its institutions and struggles as we are called to think them *sub specie infinitatis humani generis*. It is in this sense that I speak of a "spirit" of democracy: not *a* spirit that would designate a particular mentality, climate, or general postulation, but the breath that must inspire it, that in fact inspires it, so long as we know how to make it our own, which requires that we first of all be able to feel it.

The reason why political action is paralyzed today is that it can no longer be mobilized on the basis of some "prime mover" endowed with causal energy: there is no longer anything of the sort in political terms, and politics as a whole must be remobilized from elsewhere. Nor does there exist any other economic prime mover apart from capital and the growth of capital, so long, at least, as economy itself continues to be thought as what moves politics and everything else by means of the choice that values equivalence, along with an idea of "progress" that is supposed to give moral value to the indifference of this equivalence.

It is because this fundamental choice—which exercised such influence from the Renaissance through to the nineteenth century—has exhausted its virtues and so has revealed this state of exhaustion that there is no longer any political "left," even though there are more than enough reasons to become indignant and to fight, to denounce and to demand— to demand the just, lively, and beautiful infinity of man, of a man or human being beyond his rights.

· · ·

It is perhaps possible today that this choice is to be taken in a different direction. It is possible that man desires in the end nothing other than "evil": not Aristotle's "good life," which calls for a constantly renewed supplement to "life," an expansion beyond its necessity, but, on the contrary, that other supplement and that other expansion that can be brought about through the annihilation of oneself and others—as well as of the common, which is thereby reduced to a common incineration. Yes, all this is possible, and the current age of humanity has shown us a community of mass graves, famines, suicides, and degradations.

This possibility illuminates in a stunning fashion the insistent question of what I am calling here "communism" as the truth of democracy: for nothing is more *common* than the common dust to which we are all destined. Nothing is better at establishing equivalence and the definitive entropy attached to it. Nothing is more common than the death drive— and the point is not to know whether the technological politics of the state that made Auschwitz and Hiroshima possible ended up unleashing drives of this order but rather to know if a humanity weighed down by its millions of years did not choose, a couple of centuries ago, the path of its own annihilation.

But this *nihil* in annihilation, this nothing, is a substantial nothing: it is less a "common thing" (*res publica communis*) than the "common as thing, as thingified" (which, to a certain extent, "merchandise" already is). If it is this that we want, we have to know what such wanting means: not that "God is dead" but that death is becoming our God.

· · ·

Democracy means that neither death nor life has any value in and of itself, but that value comes only from shared existence insofar as it exposes itself to its absence of ultimate sense as its true—and infinite—sense of being.

If the people are sovereign, it is incumbent upon them to take responsibility for what Bataille has in mind when he writes that sovereignty is *nothing*.[10] Sovereignty is not located in any person; it has no figure, no contour; it cannot be erected into any monument. It is, simply, the supreme. With nothing above it. Neither God nor master. In this sense, democracy equals anarchy. But anarchy commits one to certain actions, operations, and struggles, to certain forms that allow one rigorously to maintain the absence of any posited, deposited, or imposed *arche*. The democratic *kratein*, the power of the people, is first of all the power to foil the *archē* and then to take responsibility, all together and each individually, for the infinite opening that is thereby brought to light.

To take responsibility for this opening means to make possible the finite inscription of the infinite. From this fundamental choice—which, it has to be repeated, is the choice of an entire civilization—results the inevitable nullification of general equivalence, which is the perpetuation of the indefinite rather than the inscription of the infinite, indifference rather than affirmative difference, tolerance rather than confrontation, gray rather than colors.

To enter into this thought is already to act. It is to be engaged in the praxis whereby what is produced is a transformed subject rather than a preformed product, an infinite subject rather than a finite object.

This praxis is the only one—coming before any reform, any reformatting, any risk management—that might engage something more than a protest and more than a revolt, namely, the dislodging of the very foundation of general equivalence and the putting into question of its false infinity.

13

Truth

Let us summarize and conclude.

The truth of democracy is the following: it is not, as it was for the ancients, one political form among others. It is not a political form at all, or
else, at the very least, it is not *first of all* a political form. That is why we
have so much trouble trying to determine it in a precise and appropriate
way, and it is also why it can appear in conformity to and homogeneous
with the domination of calculations of general equivalence and the appropriation of that equivalence (which goes by the name of "capitalism").

In its modern incarnation, democracy aimed at nothing less than the
total refoundation of politics. Whoever wants to found must first go
down deeper than the foundation. Democracy (re)engenders man,
Rousseau declares. It opens anew the destination of man and of the
world along with him. "Politics" can no longer give the measure or the
place of this destination or this *destinerrance* (Derrida). It must allow it
to be put into practice and secure multiple places for it, but it can never
assure it.

Democratic politics is thus a politics that withdraws from all assump-
tions. It cuts short every kind of "political theology," whether theocratic
or secularized. It thus posits as an axiom that not everything (including

the everything [*le tout*]) is political. That everything (or the everything) is multiple, singular-plural, the inscription in finite bursts of an infinity in actuality (where "arts," "thoughts," "loves," "gestures," "passions" would be just some of the names of these bursts).

"Democracy" is thus:

    —first of all, the name of a regime of sense whose truth cannot be subsumed under any ordering agency, whether religious, political, scientific, or aesthetic; it is, rather, that which wholly engages "man" as the risk and chance of "himself," as "dancer over the abyss," to put it in a paradoxical and deliberately Nietzschean way. This paradox brings the stakes into perfect relief: democracy is egalitarian aristocracy. This first sense borrows a political name in an only accidental and provisional way.

    —then, the duty to invent a politics *not of the ends* of the dance over the abyss, but of the means to open or to keep open the spaces of their being put to work. This distinction between ends and means is not given, no more than the distribution of possible "spaces" is. It is a matter of finding them, of inventing them, or of inventing how not even to claim to find them. But, before all else, politics must be seen as distinct from the order of ends—even if social justice clearly constitutes a necessary means to all possible ends.

Let us take a single, relatively simple example: health. It is not *given* that the criteria for health should (or could) simply be the duration or length of life or else some physiological equilibrium that would be determined on the basis of an ideal of duration or performance. The meaning of "health" cannot simply be determined in opposition to "illness" or, in general, by what medicine is for us. Medicine, illness, and health have values, senses, and modalities that depend upon profound choices made by a culture and upon an "ethos" that is anterior to all "ethics" and all "politics." A politics of health can only respond to choices and orientations that it itself can scarcely modify. (It is for this reason that the term *biopolitics* relies upon a confused hypertrophy of the sense or meaning of "politics.") A form of "health" is a thought, a grabbing hold of existence; to risk putting it in what will be judged to be a hyperbolic and archaic way—it is a metaphysics, not a politics.

The hyperbole deserves to be drawn out just a bit: democracy is first of all a metaphysics and only afterwards a politics. But the latter is not founded on the former. On the contrary, it is but the condition whereby it is exercised. If we first think the being of our being together in the world, we will see which politics gives this thought a chance. It is no doubt always possible to stretch the meaning or sense of a word, to make "politics" equal "metaphysics": but one then loses or blurs a distinction whose very principle must be consubstantial with *democracy*. This principle removes from the order of the state—without taking away anything from the functions that belong to it—the assumption of the ends of man, of common and singular existence.

THE SENSES OF DEMOCRACY

The Senses of Democracy

As a certain democratic conviction comes to be affirmed more or less everywhere, we come to ask ourselves more and more about the fragility of democracy. When it is taken for granted in every discourse that "democracy" is the only kind of political regime deemed acceptable by a humanity that has come of age, that has been emancipated, and that has no other end than itself, then the very idea of democracy loses its luster, becomes murky, and leaves us perplexed.

We must first understand that it was already from out of this murkiness which spread across Europe that we saw the emergence of all the "totalitarian" possibilities experienced during this last century. Unlike those who, in the 1920s and 1930s, could believe in the need for a radical reform of the public and the common, we ourselves are no longer able to ignore the traps or the monsters hidden behind all these perplexities with regard to democracy.

It is thus impossible to be simply "democratic" without asking what this means, for the sense of this term never stops posing difficulties, almost at every turn, indeed, every time we have recourse to it. Failure to recognize these difficulties—something quite common in political discourse—is as dangerous as the repudiation of democracy: it prevents us from thinking and thus conceals the same traps and monsters, or others still.

I shall put forward here little more than a minimal argument or schematic protocol in order to question the possible meaning or sense of "democracy."

This word can thus designate first of all the exercise of political power by the people. In this case, "the people" can itself be understood in one of two ways. It can refer to a part of the social whole that is distinct from at least one other part, to which it is considered to be inferior and to whose domination it is subjected. Here democracy is not a regime but an uprising against the regime (or at least against the government). It is the revolt of destitution, of what is intolerable in minds and bodies, the revolt of hunger and fear. The subjected thus go from being passive subjects to becoming active ones. The legitimacy of the revolt is absolute. It is, however, the legitimacy only of the revolt and is not enough to found a regime. In the revolt there are democrats but not democracy. The revolt exists only in its own act, in its own times and places. It is no accident that the idea of a "permanent revolution" was able to form what might be characterized as a vanishing point of infinite demand in modern political experience. The subject of revolt suggests two things at once: in the immediacy of the moment, an absolute, unprescribable, indivisible dignity, a value that can be measured against nothing other than itself, and, over time, the same absolute value as an infinite opening that no quality, law, institution, or even identity can ever bring to a close. Democratic politics is thus a politics of periodic return to the breach [*brèche*] of the revolt. It can determine the circumstances and the subject that open this breach only on a case by case basis.

By contrast, "the people" can also be understood as the whole [*le tout*] and the body, as it were, of social reality. Instead of a differential thinking, we have here an integral thinking. The political sovereignty of the people thus means before all else the people's self-constitution as a people. This self-constitution obviously precedes any political constitution, where the people are constituting, not constituted. Here the subject-people is affirmed not as an actor or as a force but first of all as a substance: a reality that derives its existence and its movement only from itself. The history of modern thought shows two things: either the impossibility of engendering a politics that would be the self-engendering of the people ("direct" democracy, the infinite presupposition of a common will and organicity: what Rousseau declares to be good only for the gods), or else the resolution of the democratic problem through the dissolution of the entire political sphere as one distinct sphere among others, which disappears in a total and self-producing social existence (Marx).

Once this first hypothesis has been taken fully into account, as our history seems to have done, two possible modalities follow for what might be called a politics in negativity: either the periodic and dispersed politics of those singular configurations of the "breach," something that also implies abstention from participation in democratic institutions (parliamentary and republican)—or else a thinking of democracy that follows the impossibility of incarnating the essence of democracy and of representing its figure, alongside the necessity of "democratically" keeping open this impossibility. In both cases, politics is affirmed in an essential way through a withdrawal [*retrait*], in the sense, precisely, that the political, as the subsumptive unity of nature and destiny, or project and identity, for something like a "people" must be held in withdrawal from itself, the negative index of a presence that is always at a remove. This is the model of negative theology, and, indeed, it is a matter here only of politics as onto-theo-political (or as the "theologico-political"), the sign of which has simply been inverted. (The question might thus be formulated in this way: Have revolutions done anything other than invert the sign of theologico-political transcendence?)

But "democracy" can also designate not only something expressly political but "civil society" or the "social bond," considered from the point of view of an ethos or a democratic feeling under the regulative idea represented by the motto "liberty, equality, fraternity," however this is to be interpreted. In this respect, democracy is a description and/or an evaluation of a being in common founded upon the mutual recognition of fellows [*semblables*] and upon the independence of each group wherein this recognition is shared. The model for such a group is given in the form of what is called a "commune" (as in Tocqueville) or a "community" (as in Marx). Two ways of thinking the commun(ity) are thus possible.

In the first (which is more American, according to Tocqueville), the commune is not yet in the realm of the political: it is before the state and can be represented as existing without it or beneath it; its freedom is more of an emancipation [*franchise*] than a self-constituting freedom. It is local and restricted; it does not involve power as such. It is a kind of interiority, and its exterior is as much the other commune as the state itself, which thus appears less as an agency of subsumption and identification than as a quite separate agency in charge of another sphere (an imperial or federal power).

In the second (more European and differentiated into a variety of socialist or fascist forms), the community takes the place of the negativity formulated above. Its interiority or subjectivity takes on the identificatory and subsumptive role of the state, which tends to efface or sublimate itself within it. A positive onto-theologico-political is thus reconstituted, but in an immanent and no longer transcendent version.

It thus seems that the question of democracy can be summed up in the following way: Does this word ultimately designate the reconfiguration of the theologico-political through a transcendent-negative or positive-immanent metamorphosis, or does it designate a genuine break with the theologico-political? (It is not hard to see here the general outline of the debate over "secularism" that opposed Carl Schmitt and Hans Blumenberg. Generally speaking, it is a debate over the essence or the sense of modernity.)

If, as I believe, it is indeed a matter of a break, it is nonetheless appropriate to determine in what way it has not yet been completed. Not only does the "European" thinking of democracy often remain weighed down by a political theology (whether positive or negative), but the "American" thinking at once unleashes the forces of inequality, which are no longer tempered by an "inner" principle of the "people," and leads to various kinds of communitarian retreat, each at once sterile in itself and incompatible with all the others. There thus remains at least one sense of "democracy" (or whatever name you want to give it) that has not yet been elaborated. (The designations "European" and "American" are, here, formal indications: the real characteristics take shape, to some extent, everywhere. It is nonetheless not incongruous to think that Europe, in spite of all its shortcomings, might indeed be a place for putting to the test a truly new sense of "democracy.")

The task that is clearly set forth is thus neither a destruction of democracy nor its indefinite perfecting: it is above all to decide on the "break" in question and thus on "modernity" (or what is called "post-modernity"). This decision will require a decision about the nature, stakes, and place of politics. Must politics still be thought under the aegis of the theologico-political (or of what is simply called today "the political")? Or must it be thought in relation to an essential *withdrawal* or *retreat* [retrait] of this "political" (essential, substantial, and subsumptive of all being in common)? This retreat would be not a retirement or a retiring but a retracing of everything that being in common is (being together or being with). In a singular fashion, it would be a matter of knowing whether the political sphere must not remain distinct from the sphere of the "common," which it would neither exhaust nor command from above. Politics is not responsible for the identity and destiny of the common, but only for the regulation—even if it is infinite—of justice. (It thus has to do with power.) The common, however, puts existence in play. (It thus has to do with sense.) What is at stake here is a separation between sense and power. One certainly does not exclude the other, but one cannot replace the other, either. (This does not undermine the legitimacy of revolt, but it does displace its ultimate horizon.) The theologico-political subsumes at once power and sense, justice and existence; it absorbs the common into the political (or vice versa). Ultimately, one no longer knows what "common" or "political" means. That is what is so perplexing about "democracy." It is thus a matter of thinking the interval between the common and the political: we do not belong to the one as we do to the other, and "everything" is not "political." And "everything" is not common either, since the "common" is neither a thing nor an everything, that is, a whole [un tout]. Between power and sense there is proximity and distancing, at once—altogether—a relation of power and a relation of sense . . . It is perhaps a completely new form of man's relationship to himself, where man would no longer be "his own end" (if such is indeed the basis of democracy) unless he were able to distance himself from himself in order to go beyond.

IS EVERYTHING POLITICAL?

Is Everything Political?

(a simple note)

There is a phrase floating on the horizon of our thinking that says that *everything is political.* This phrase can be pronounced or understood in several different ways: either in a distributive mode (where the different moments or elements of common existence all derive in some way from the moment or element called "political," which itself then occupies a privileged position of diffusion or transversality), or in a mode of domination (where, in the first or the last instance, it is the "political" sphere that determines or governs the activity of all other spheres), or else, finally, in an integrative or assumptive mode (where the essence of the whole of existence is political in nature). In each case, the tone of the pronouncement or of the reception can be resigned, disconcerted, affirmative, or demanding.

But before simply and vaguely "floating" there on the horizon, this phrase was the axiom for an entire modern elaboration. It no doubt constituted and consolidated the horizon itself during a very long period—from 1789, perhaps, right up to our own time, though we ourselves are unable to determine whether "our own time" is still circumscribed by this horizon. (This phrase was also, however, a verdict or a slogan for various fascisms as well as communisms: despite their many differences, it was no doubt also their point of contact.)

So as not to linger, in this brief note, on what will have preceded modernity, let us be content to suggest the following: politics was never "totalizing" for the ancients, who no doubt invented politics but who thought it only in the context of a city of "free men," that is, in the context of an essentially differential and not "totalizing" city. Slavery alone, together with its economic corrolates, prevents us from understanding, for example, the "architectonic" place of politics in Aristotle along the lines of a thought such as "everything is political." In this political space, a free man enjoys his life in the polis for ends other than those of political organization (for example, the *bios theoretikos*, the leisure of the contemplative life), just as the polis is sustained by infra-political foundations (slavery and a subsistence made possible primarily through family units). The politics of sovereign nation-states, for its part, was sustained through a relationship to a destination common to all and for each alone that always went beyond politics in one way or another (a religious or symbolic destination)—although, in another sense, this same sovereignty led to a "politics in totality" that became that of the moderns.

. . .

If it is sometimes said today that politics is held in check or marginalized by economy, this is due to a willful confusion: what is called "economy" is in fact nothing other than what used to be called "political economy," that is, the management of subsistence and prosperity on the scale not of the family, which is relatively self-sufficient (the *oikos*, the household), but of the city-state (*polis*). "Political economy" was nothing other than a consideration of the *polis* as an *oikos*: as a collective or communitarian reality that supposedly belonged to a natural order (generation, kinship, inheritance and patrimony: land, goods, slaves). It logically followed that, if *oiko-nomia* was to be thought on the scale of the *polis*, the displacement could not simply be one of magnitude; it also implied that the *politeia*, that is, a knowledge of the affairs of the city-state, had to be reinterpreted as an *oiko-nomia*. But the latter was at the same time reinterpreted no longer only in terms of subsistence and prosperity (of "the good life") but in terms of the production and reproduction of wealth (of "having more").

In the end, it is always a question of the way in which the grouping together of men gets interpreted. It is understood as "wholly political" so long as the "political" is determined as total, totalizing, all-encompassing or en-globing. And that is indeed what happened, in a major way, when it came to be determined as the globality of an *oikos*: more precisely, as an *oiko-logical* globality, that is, as the concurrence or coming together of the natural resources of its members. This was originally called "physiocracy" ("government by nature").

At the same time, it was necessary to determine the "natural" nature of the members of the political *oikos*: this was done by constituting the city-state no longer on the basis of an order that was autonomous and transcendent in relationship to the *oikoi* (founding or federating them while having an essence different from theirs) but on the basis of a supposedly originary "oikology," an originary famil(y)iarity amongst men and between them and nature. Hence the institution of a "social body" or of a "civil society" (in the first and precise sense of this term: a political society or society of citizens) was given as basically, ideally, or originally identical to the institution or founding of humanity itself. Humanity itself, then, would have no final destination other than its own self-production as a second nature or as a totally humanized nature (assuming that such a concept is not a contradiction in terms, though this is no doubt one of the cruxes of the problem . . .).

According to this logic, "everything is political" is assumed from the start, and it then follows that "politics" itself, as the separate order of a particular institution, knowledge, or art, can only tend toward the suppression of its own separation so as to realize the natural totality that it expresses or first of all indicates. In this respect, there is in the final analysis no difference between "everything is political" and "everything is economic." That is how democracy and the market can follow a common path in the process that is today known as "globalization." "Everything is political" thus also amounts to affirming that there is a self-sufficiency of "man" considered as the producer of his own nature and, through it, of nature in its entirety. Today the vague or ill-defined representation of this self-sufficiency and this self-production continues to dominate the representations of "politics" from both the "right" and the "left," all those, at least, that present themselves under the banner of a global political "project," be it "for the state" or "against the state," "consensual" or "revolutionary." (There also exists a weak version of this, where politics acts merely to regulate and correct imbalances and defuse tensions: but the motivation behind this "social-democratic" tinkering, while sometimes quite honorable—even if often burdened by compromises—remains nonetheless the same.)

. . .

The only question posed by what is today called the "crisis," "eclipse," or "paralysis" of politics is thus, in the end, that of man's self-sufficiency and/or of the nature that is within him or that comes about through him. It is precisely this self-sufficiency that is being shown to be more and more inconsistent with each passing day. For globalization—or the general oiko-logization of the polis—makes apparent in an ever more vivid or violent manner the *non-naturality* of its own process (but also, ultimately, that of this supposed "nature" itself: never have we been so much in the order of a *meta-physis*).

This "man" who freed himself through the "eco-political in totality," the "man" whose social market represents simultaneously and symmetrically the universal form of "rights" and the planetary proliferation of injustices, extortions, and exploitations, turns out to be not so much "alienated" (where the "proper" would designate that in relation to which an "alienation" might be determined and measured) as altogether lacking in identity, property, end, and measure. Man bears witness first of all to a lack of being [*manque à être*]. On the one hand, those who are exploited, the have-nots, who are reduced simply to having to survive, are prohibited from existing (it is indeed a *prohibition* rather than a lack), while, on the other hand, the "haves" know ever more acutely—beyond all compassion—that neither their well-being nor the corresponding ill-being of those others produces any being-human [*l'être-homme*] or any being-world [*l'être-monde*].

But it is no doubt this "lack"—and this would be the most recent lesson, still almost inaudible, unheard of—that reveals at the same time the insufficiency of a simple logic of lack: such a logic, analogous to a logic of alienation, presupposes a "plenitude" as *terminus a quo* or *ad quem*. But if there is no *terminus*—no end or origin—it is because of the paradoxical logic of a complete incompletion or an infinite finitude. This logic turns out henceforth to constitute "man" and with him (and through him) "nature" as well as "history." The invention of the *politeia* thus reveals itself, perhaps, to have already been, in the singular light of this paradox, the bringing to light of such a logic. The man of *logos*, the one who is properly the *zōon politikon*, is the being whose proper measure is incommensurable and inappropriable. The polis represented itself simultaneously as a given common measure, or as the self-donation of a common measure, *and* as an indefinite instability and a permanent reelaboration (even if the manifestations of this are rather rare and episodic) of the measure of the incommensurable. (The index of the "common measure" is then to be understood at once in a transversal sense, where the measure constitutes the bond, and in a distributive sense, where the measure is meted out to each one.)

The measure has a name: justice. Insofar as it is not given, justice entails the exercise of a power (and thus of counter-powers, the overthrowing of power, alliances of power, and so on). The exercise of such power, however we imagine it, is from the outset incompatible with an identification under some *oiko-nomia*, that is, under some natural self-sufficiency. But it has become obvious that there is no oikonomia: there is, no matter how you look at it, only an *ecotechnē*, that is, a common place or place of habitation within production, the invention and incessant transformation of ends that are never given. Never, no doubt, has the domination of "political economy" been more crushing: but never has the fundamental inconsistency of its "self-sufficiency" been more evident. Never has it been more evident that *value*, absolutely speaking (the value of "man" or that of the "world") is absolutely incommensurable with every other measured (evaluated) value. (Commensurability is called "general equivalence.")

. . .

Politics has withdrawn as the donation (the auto- or hetero-donation, whether human or divine) of a common essence and destination: it has withdrawn as totality or as totalization. In this sense, not everything is political. But politics can still be retraced as the place of the exercise of power in view of an incommensurable justice—that is, as the place for claiming an in-finity of being man and being world. By definition, it does not absorb into itself all the other places of existence. These other places are where incommensurability is in some way *formed* and *presented*: they can go by the names "art," "religion," "thought," "science," "ethics," "conduct," "exchange," "production," "love," "war," "kinship," "intoxi-cation"—and the list could go on ad infinitum: their respective distinc-tions and circumscriptions (which do not prevent certain contiguities or intersections) each time point out the occurrence of a configuration ac-cording to which a certain presentation takes place—even if this presen-tation gives form to an impresentation or to a withdrawal of presence. (These nonpolitical spheres are not, however, those of a "private" as op-posed to a "public" order: all spheres are public and private, if we want to use these terms. They are *shared [out]*, in the double-edged sense of this term.) Between these configurations (but without forgetting, once again, their points of contact and contagion), there is incommensurabil-ity. Politics is reconfigured in this place: as the place where it is a matter of keeping this incommensurability open, the incommensurability of justice as well as that of value. Contrary to what was asserted by the the-ologico-political as well as by political economy—though not without relation to what was at stake in that polis "before politics" (so to speak)— politics is no longer the place of an assumption of unitotality. Nor is it a place for the putting into form or the putting into presence of incom-mensurability or some kind of unity of origin and end, that is, in short, of a "humanity." Politics is in charge of space and of spacing (of space-time), but it is not in charge of figuring.

To be sure, politics is the place of an "in common" as such—but only along the lines of an incommensurability that is kept open (and in accordance with the two axes sketched out above). It does not subsume the "in common" under any kind of union, community, subject, or epiphany. Everything that is of the "common" is not political, and what is political is not in every way "common." But at the same time, neither the sphere of the "in common" nor that of politics allows for the separation between "society as exteriority" and "community as interiority." (This dualism works no better for the social body/soul than it does for the individual one.)

From now on, politics must be understood as the specific place for the articulation of a nonunity—and for the symbolization of a nonfigure. The words *equality* and *freedom* are but problematic names, nonsaturated by signification, under which it is a matter of keeping open (dare one say wide open?) the exigency of *not* accomplishing an essence or an end of the incommensurable, and *yet*, and *precisely*, of sustaining its (im)possibility: the exigency to regulate power—the force that must sustain this nonorganic nonunity—according to an incommensurable "justice." The exigency, therefore, of regulating according to a universal that is not given and must be produced. In such a place, politics is far from being "everything"—even though everything passes through it and meets up or crosses paths in it. Politics becomes precisely a place of detotalization. Or, one might venture to say: *if* "*everything is political*"—*in a sense that is neither that of political theology nor of political economy*—*it is insofar as the* "*everything*" *[le* "*tout*"*] can be neither total nor totalized in any way.* Can one think "democracy" at such a height or with such intensity?

Notes

1. Nancy is no doubt referring to the campaign speech of Nicolas Sarkozy of April 29, 2007. Speaking to his supporters in Paris just days before the final round of elections he would go on to win to become president of France, Sarkozy condemned the "legacy" of May 68 as having "introduced cynicism into society and into politics" and as having "imposed an intellectual and moral relativism . . . where there is no difference between good and evil, truth and falsity, the beautiful and the ugly." Arguing that "the legacy of May 68 had weakened the authority of the state" by "denigrating national identity and igniting hatred for the family, society, the State, the Nation, and the Republic," Sarkozy concluded that he wished "to turn the page on May 68" and bring back to politics the morality and the "idea of citizenship" that May 68 had taken out of it.—Trans.

2. The "March 22 Movement" was a student protest movement that began on March 22, 1968, at Nanterre University, outside of Paris, and quickly spread across France. The movement was in part a protest against American imperialism in Vietnam and in part a challenge to French traditions and authorities, including those of the French university system and the French government. Daniel Cohn-Bendit and Alain Geismar, both students at Nanterre, were the principal organizers of the movement.—Trans.

3. That is, 1789, the beginning of the French Revolution; 1848, the revolution that established the Second Republic in France; and 1917, the Russian Revolution.—Trans.

4. The CFDT, or the Confédération Française Démocratique du Travail, is France's largest labor union.—Trans.

5. Martin Heidegger, "The Age of the World Picture," in *The Question Concerning Technology and Other Essays*, ed. and trans. William Lovitt (New York: Harper Torchbooks, 1977), 115–54.—Trans.

6. That is why "communism" must not be put forward as a "hypothesis," as we see in Alain Badiou—a political hypothesis that is then to be verified by a kind of political action that is itself caught in the schema of a classic struggle—but must instead be posited as a given, as a fact: our first given. Before all else, we are in common. Then we must become what we are: the given is an exigency, and this exigency is infinite.

7. "Know then, proud man, what a paradox you are to yourself. Be humble, impotent reason! Be silent, feeble nature! Learn that man infinitely transcends man [*l'homme passe infiniment l'homme*], hear from your master your true condition, which is unknown to you" (Blaise Pascal, *Pensées*, trans. A. J. Krailsheimer [Baltimore: Penguin Books, 1966], no. 131/434).—Trans.

8. When one speaks of "political theology," especially when one uses the adjective "theologico-political," one usually produces, due to a distortion of the meaning of these words in Carl Schmitt, their inventor, a certain confusion: one wishes to designate an alliance between, if not a fusion of, two registers, in short, a theocracy, there where, on the contrary, a very clear distinction exists. Clarification: Spinoza's *Tractatus theologico-politicus* has nothing at all to do with what Schmitt calls "political theology." Quite the contrary.

9. Aristotle defines the polis as existing not for the sake of life but for the "good life [*eu zēn*]" in book 1 of his *Politics*.—Trans.

10. In and of itself, this qualification does not go against the political principle of sovereignty as articulated from Bodin (or even Machiavelli) to Carl Schmitt. In this tradition, sovereignty is nothing—nothing but its own exercise. But this very exercise makes sense and accomplishes a destination for a people, even if this destination leads in turn only to a succession of imposing and perishable figures of this people. But in this case, the *noth-*

ing is not being taken absolutely seriously, and it is from religion, or else from nihilism, that we end up borrowing the final word. Democracy requires, on the contrary, that there be no final word and that the *nothing*—since there is no other world—be taken absolutely seriously, in the infinity it opens right in the midst of finitude.